THANK YOU FOR YOUR CONTINUED SUPPORT.

Thank you for your continued support.

Copyright © 2022
Published in 2025 by My Littl' Workshop
Contributing artist For the cover Prince Jai

To purchase additional copies of this book, visit Amazon or www.MyLittlWorkshop.com.

All rights reserved. No part of this book/journal may be reproduced, distributed, or transmitted in any form or by any means, including electronic, mechanical, photocopying, recording, or by any information storage and retrieval system, without prior written permission from the copyright owner, author, or publisher (MyLittlWorkshop.com).

My Littl' Workshop proudly supports the Sista Foundation Inc., a nonprofit organization dedicated to empowering young women, mentoring young men, and strengthening communities through workshops and social events.

NAME:

CONTACT:

YEAR:

GIFT FROM:

EMERGENCY:

OTHER INFO:

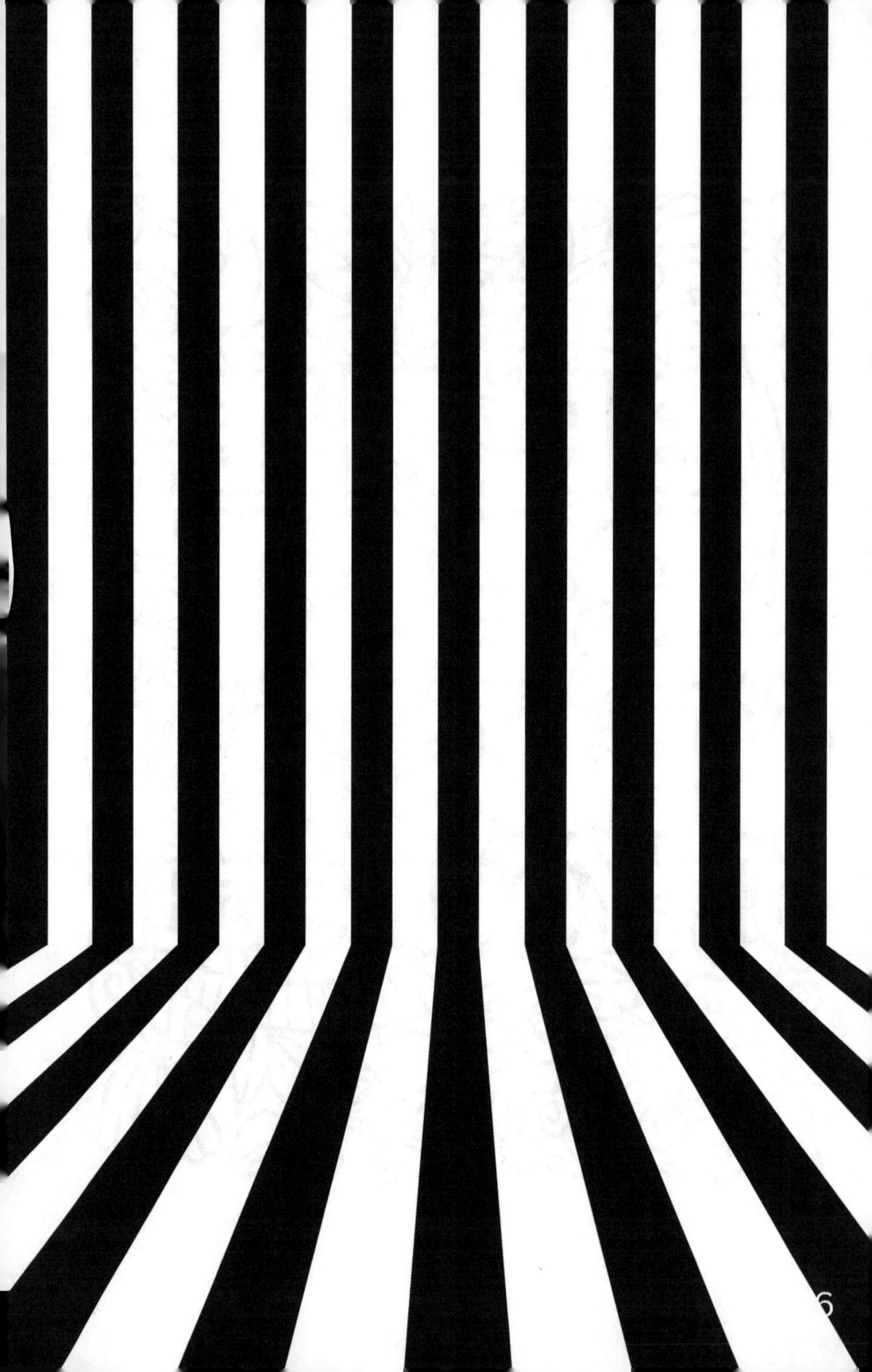

MONEY LOVES TO SERVE ME

MONEY FOLLOWS ME WHEREVER I GO

MONEY PRECEDES ME WHOLEHEARTEDLY

MONEY IS SO HAPPY WITH ME THAT IT COMES TO ME NONSTOP.

Say it LOUD:
I LOOK LIKE MONEY

Money loves to support me
PEOPLE LOVE TO SHARE THEIR MONEY WITH ME

Money always finds me
MONEY LOVES TO SERVE ME

You are not here by accident

"If you're reading this, it means you have an interest in money. Maybe you desire more, dream of abundance, or are simply in need of a financial breakthrough. Perhaps you've been going through tough times, trying countless methods that haven't worked, and now here you are, taking another chance. But let me tell you — this isn't a chance on just anything; it's a chance on yourself.

Within these pages, I'll share tools and insights with you, but it will be up to you to use, remix, and make them your own. If you truly want to bring money into your life, you must first learn to respect her. Yes, money is a 'her,' and she requires the same reverence and respect you'd give any powerful, feminine force in your life. If you ignore her or mistreat her, she'll slip away, only giving you a little here and there to keep herself alive. But if you embrace her with respect, she'll stay, she'll grow, and she'll give you what you deserve.

People often set boundaries for themselves, and limit their talents, their power, and their potential, while letting everything else walk all over them. This is your reminder that you don't have to live that way. You deserve to have the amount of money you desire, to enjoy the life you dream of, to help the people you care about, and to live on your own terms.

Imagine yourself like Daniel standing before the lions. You have the power to turn it from a threat into a companion, a protector, and a force that works for you. You can either keep hiding, or you can walk up to your lion — to your money — and make it serve you. The choice is yours. So, let this be the day you decide to rise up, respect yourself, respect money, and create the life you've always wanted."

I am aware that this statement on the previous page is very bold but also has an empowering tone for the rest of the book, encouraging you to shift your mindset and take ownership of your relationship with money.

My question to you this instant is....

I just want to be straight to the point, as I know that this is not necessarily a dissertation or some fancy paper that I am writing but rather something to stir your soul, support your spirit, change your mind, and expand your awareness. This is why my introduction is direct, spiritually grounded, and empowering.

It sets a bold tone, encouraging readers, and in the near future listeners, to challenge old beliefs and step into a new mindset where abundance and wealth are their rightful inheritance. It's a powerful call to action, inviting them to embrace a fresh perspective and commit to this transformative journey.

Read what you read, trust what you trust, and believe in what you believe in. If you dare, read Psalms 23 and 27, and let's get to work.

2 Corinthians 9:8: 'And God will generously provide all you need.' Why won't you just go with that flow? It does not mean that you're not going to work and stay stagnant but it means that you have back up so accept it. You are not alone. You are not abandoned.

Somewhere along the line, someone told you a different story — that you were born into poverty, that wealth wasn't meant for you — and you believed it. That story became your truth, and now every time you hear something that challenges it, you're ready to reject it. You feel triggered, therefore, you put your guard up so you can never learn the truth, but instead, you're stuck in the abyss of one lie after another.

But today, I challenge you to begin this journey by accepting a new truth: that wealth is your birthright. It's yours, and you shall see it before you cross to the other side. My only question to you is: Are you willing? Are you willing to accept a new truth? Are you willing to unlearn so you can learn, and relearn?

For now, let's get to work. Welcome to The Money Love Affair!"

Welcome to something NEW

This passage is a powerful reminder to set a clear intention and commit to personal growth on your own terms, rather than simply chasing what others have achieved. It emphasizes the importance of respecting and developing our own unique gifts and staying disciplined in our craft. This journey is not for the faint-hearted; it demands dedication, especially in fields that require late nights, quiet contemplation, and deep connection with the unseen forces around us.

The message also touches on the rare and sacred knowledge that comes in moments of solitude, particularly in the stillness of early dawn or the late hours when distractions fade. It invites you to open your heart and mind to insights that can only be accessed in those quiet moments when the world sleeps and whispers of wisdom become audible to those who are ready to receive.

Ultimately, it's a call to action: to honor your own journey, respect the gifts that are uniquely yours, and step into the unknown with courage. Welcome to a world where dedication to personal growth, discipline, and openness to the whispers of inspiration will lead you to true success.

What Money is & isn't

Money is a tool
Never a fool
Money is not a Master
But a great servant

Money is both a tool and a symbol, existing in physical and conceptual forms, that enables the exchange of value. Its primary purpose is to act as a medium of exchange, a store of value, and a unit of account, facilitating the buying and selling of goods, services, and labor within economies. But beyond its economic function, money also carries cultural, emotional, psychological, and spiritual meanings, depending on the perspective you adopt.

Let's explore the different ways to understand what money is:

1. Money as a Medium of Exchange

At its most basic, money allows people to trade and exchange goods and services without needing a barter system (where goods are directly exchanged for other goods). Instead of trading livestock for grain, for example, money serves as a universally accepted form of exchange. This makes transactions smoother and less complicated.

- Example: You go to a grocery store and buy food using cash, a debit card, or digital currency. The store accepts your money in exchange for goods because they know they can use that money to buy other things.

2. Money as a Store of Value

Money holds value over time, meaning it can be saved and used in the future. Unlike perishable items like food or flowers, money (especially in its modern form) doesn't spoil. As long as inflation remains low, the value stored in money remains relatively stable over time.

- Example: If you save $100 today, you can use that same $100 next month or next year to buy something of roughly equal value (depending on inflation and market factors).

3. Money as a Unit of Account

Money allows us to measure and compare the value of different things in a common metric. For example, rather than saying a cow is worth ten chickens, we assign a monetary value to both the cow and the chickens.

- Example: You can compare the price of a car, a house, or a meal at a restaurant in terms of dollars (or your local currency) to determine how much they are worth relative to one another.

4. Money as Energy and Flow (Spiritual View)

From a spiritual or metaphysical perspective, money is often seen as a form of energy. It is neither inherently good nor bad; instead, it is neutral and takes on the energy we give it. When we have a healthy relationship with money, we treat it as a flow that comes into our lives to support us and flows out to support others or fund our goals. In this sense, money can be seen as an expression of your intentions, desires, and beliefs.

- Example: If you view money as something scarce or hard to obtain, you may create barriers to receiving it. If you see money as abundant and a tool to enhance your life, you may attract more of it into your life. It flows where energy and intention flow.

5. Money as a Psychological Construct

Money also holds deep psychological significance for people. How we think about money often reflects how we think about security, success, self-worth, and power. Money can trigger emotional responses like fear, greed, guilt, and even shame, depending on one's past experiences and upbringing.

- Example: Someone who grew up in poverty might have lingering anxiety about money and its scarcity, even if they become financially successful as an adult. On the other hand, a person who grew up with financial security might have a more relaxed view of money.

6. Money as a Cultural and Social Construct

Money reflects social and cultural values. Different cultures have varying beliefs about money, including how it should be used, saved, or spent. In some cultures, money is a means to gain status, power, or influence. In others, it's viewed as a communal resource or something that should be shared for the collective good.

- Example: In some communities, giving money or resources to family members or contributing to communal projects is highly valued, while in others, individual wealth accumulation is more prized.

7. Money and Freedom

For many people, money represents freedom—the freedom to make choices, travel, pursue hobbies, or provide for their loved ones. Having enough money can bring a sense of control over your life, giving you options to live according to your desires and not being restricted by financial constraints.

- Example: When you have a financial cushion or savings, you may feel more empowered to quit a job you don't enjoy or start a business you've always dreamed of.

8. Money as a Source of Responsibility
Money also represents responsibility. The more money you have, the more responsibility you often feel in terms of managing it, using it wisely, and helping others with it. Many people use their wealth to create positive changes, whether through charity, philanthropy, or supporting causes they believe in.

- Example: Wealthy individuals might start foundations or charities to address global issues, and on a smaller scale, many people budget carefully to ensure their money is used responsibly for their families and communities.

Different Forms of Money:

Physical Money: Cash, coins, and tangible money you can hold.

Digital Money: Bank balances, credit, and cryptocurrency are forms of money you can't physically touch but are just as valid in today's economy.

Barter and Trade: Even though most people use money, trading goods and services directly without money can still exist in some communities or as part of personal exchanges.

Cryptocurrency: Digital assets like Bitcoin, Ethereum, or other blockchain-based currencies that challenge traditional forms of money.

In Summary, Money Is:
- A practical tool for exchange, storage, and measurement of value.

- An energetic flow that reflects your mindset, beliefs, and emotional connection to wealth.

- A psychological mirror that reveals your attitudes toward security, self-worth, and power.

- A societal force that shapes how communities interact, grow, and thrive.

- A source of freedom and responsibility that can influence the direction and quality of your life.

The relationship you cultivate with money can impact nearly every area of your life, including your sense of self, your opportunities, and your ability to give to others. Embracing money as a neutral, positive force that can serve your greater purpose—rather than a source of fear or limitation—can allow you to invite more abundance into your life with ease.

Try to explore any specific aspects of this relationship further so you can better understand where you are coming from in your own relationship with money.

To develop the right mindset about money

To develop the right mindset about money, it's essential to shift your thoughts, beliefs, and habits in ways that align with financial abundance, responsibility, and a healthy relationship with wealth. Here's a step-by-step guide to cultivating the right mindset about money:

1. Understand Your Current Money Beliefs

Your mindset about money is often rooted in your past experiences, upbringing, and cultural influences. To change your mindset, you first need to understand where your current beliefs come from.

Reflect on your childhood experiences: How did your parents or guardians talk about and manage money? Did you hear phrases like "money doesn't grow on trees" or "we can't afford that"? These messages shape how you think about money today.

Examine your current financial habits: Are you a saver, an investor, or a spender? Do you avoid looking at your finances because it causes you stress? Your behaviors reflect your underlying beliefs.

2. Release Limiting Beliefs About Money

Limiting beliefs are negative ideas or assumptions about money that block you from achieving financial abundance. Common limiting beliefs include:

> "Money is the root of all evil."
> "Rich people are greedy."
> "I'll never have enough."
> "I don't deserve wealth."

These beliefs limit your ability to attract and manage money effectively. To shift your mindset:
Identify your limiting beliefs. Write down any negative thoughts you have about money. Challenge those beliefs. Ask yourself, "Is this really true?" Often, limiting beliefs are based on fears or societal conditioning rather than facts. Replace them with empowering beliefs. For example, replace "I'll never have enough" with "Money is abundant, and there is more than enough for me."

3. Embrace an Abundance Mindset
If you reject an abundance mindset yet are trying to get abundant, it's like trying to fit a camel through the eye of the needle. An abundance mindset means believing that there is more than enough money and resources for everyone. It's the opposite of a scarcity mindset, which focuses on lack and competition.

- Visualize abundance: See yourself living in financial freedom, able to do the things you love without stress. Picture your life in detail—how it feels, what you do with your time, and how you contribute to others.
- Practice gratitude: Focus on the wealth you already have. Being grateful for your current financial situation (no matter how modest) signals to your subconscious mind that you are already abundant and open to receiving more.
- Recognize that money flows: Money isn't static—it flows in and out. Understand that even when you spend money, or better yet invest money, you're participating in an energetic flow, and more will come back to you when you maintain the right energy and actions.

Date:

Identify your limiting beliefs. Write down any negative thoughts you have about money.

Date:

Challenge those beliefs.

4. Develop a Growth Mindset About Wealth

A growth mindset, coined by psychologist Carol Dweck, means believing that your abilities and circumstances can improve through effort and learning. This applies to money as well.

- **Learn about money:** Financial literacy is key to developing a positive money mindset. Read books, take courses, or listen to podcasts about managing money, investing, and wealth-building. The more you understand money, the more empowered you'll feel.
- **Focus on solutions:** If you face a financial setback, don't dwell on the problem. Instead, ask, "What can I do to fix this?" Shifting your focus to solutions helps you take control of your financial situation. So focus on solutions-based approaches.
- **Stay open to opportunities:** Whether it's a side hustle, a new job, or an investment, being open to financial growth opportunities will help you grow your wealth over time.

5. Change How You Talk About Money

Your language about money can reinforce either a scarcity or abundance mindset. Be mindful of how you speak about wealth.

- **Avoid negative statements:** Eliminate phrases like "I'm broke," "I can't afford that," or "I'll never be rich." These statements reinforce lack and poverty.

Use positive affirmations: Create a list of empowering money affirmations, such as:

- "Money flows to me easily and effortlessly."
- "I am worthy of financial abundance."
- "I manage money wisely, and money supports my goals."
- "There is always more than enough."

Repeat these affirmations daily to reprogram your subconscious beliefs about money.

6. Set Clear Financial Goals

To cultivate the right mindset about money, you need a clear sense of direction for your finances. Setting specific, achievable financial goals helps you focus your energy on what you want to accomplish.

- Break goals into short-term and long-term: Whether it's paying off debt, saving for a house, or investing in a business, clearly define your financial goals and create an actionable plan to achieve them.

- Visualize achieving your goals: Imagine the feeling of accomplishing each financial milestone. The more vividly you can picture success, the more motivated and aligned your mindset will be.

- Track your progress: Keeping track of your financial growth, no matter how small, reinforces the idea that you're moving toward financial abundance.

Date:

Create a list of empowering money affirmations:

7. Surround Yourself with Financial Positivity

The people and environments you surround yourself with can have a significant influence on your money mindset.

- Learn from financially successful people: Whether it's through books, podcasts, or mentorship, surround yourself with people who have a positive relationship with money. Their beliefs and strategies will inspire and influence your own.

- Limit exposure to financial negativity: Avoid spending, or investing, too much time with people who constantly complain about money or focus on lack. Instead, engage with those who view money as a tool for growth and opportunity.

8. Practice Mindfulness and Gratitude

Being mindful about money helps you develop a deeper awareness of your financial habits and thoughts.

- Mindful spending (investing): Before making a purchase, ask yourself, "Does this align with my financial goals? Does it bring me value or joy?" Mindful spending (investing) helps prevent impulsive buys and aligns your money with your values.

- Practice gratitude daily: Write down three things you are grateful for regularly in your journal, including the financial blessings you already have. This keeps your mindset focused on abundance rather than lack.

Date:

Write down three to seven things you are grateful for, including the financial blessings you already have in your life.

9. Shift Your Perception of Wealth

Many people associate wealth with materialism or greed, but money is simply a tool that magnifies who you already are. If you are a kind, generous person, wealth will give you more resources to contribute positively to the world.

- See money as a means to an end: Understand that money is not the end goal, but rather a resource to help you live the life you desire—whether that's traveling, giving back to your community, or supporting your family.
- Focus on value creation: Shift from a mindset of "how can I get more money" to "how can I create value for others?" When you focus on contributing value through your work, business, or relationships, money will naturally flow to you as a result of that value.

10. Give Back and Circulate Wealth

Part of having a healthy money mindset is recognizing that money should flow both in and out. Giving back—whether through donations, supporting causes, or helping others—reinforces the flow of abundance.

- Give without fear of lack: When you give, you affirm that there is enough for everyone, and you trust that more will come to you in return. This strengthens your abundance mindset and creates a positive relationship with money.
- Share your financial success: Use your wealth to contribute to others' lives, whether through mentoring, offering advice, or helping your community grow financially.

Conclusion: The Right Money Mindset

The right mindset about money is one that combines abundance, gratitude, and financial literacy. It's about releasing fear, scarcity, and limiting beliefs while embracing the opportunities money offers. When you view money as a tool for growth and a natural flow of energy that supports your goals, you will cultivate a mindset that attracts wealth, encourages wise financial decisions, and helps you live a more prosperous life.

The journey toward a healthy money mindset is ongoing, but with awareness and intention, you can reshape your relationship with wealth. Would you like to explore any part of this mindset shift in more detail?

Developing the Right Mindset About Money & Understanding its Spiritual Connection.

To cultivate a positive and abundant relationship with money, it's essential to understand both the mindset and the spiritual aspects of money. Money is more than just a tool for survival or a symbol of wealth—it is energy, a resource that flows and magnifies who we are and how we contribute to the world.

Here's how to develop a healthy mindset about money and align with its spiritual essence:

1. Recognize Money as Energy
At its core, money is a form of energy. Just like any other type of energy, it flows in and out of our lives based on how we interact with it. Money has no inherent morality—it's neither "good" nor "evil." Instead, it amplifies the intentions behind it.

- Shift your perception: See money as a neutral tool that reflects your values, actions, and mindset. It can be a means to create positive change and support your goals.

- Understand the energetic exchange: When you give money, you aren't losing it—you're circulating energy that will flow back to you in different forms. Similarly, when you receive money, you are part of a larger energetic cycle of giving and receiving.

2. Release Limiting Beliefs

Your financial reality is often shaped by the beliefs you've inherited or internalized about money. Limiting beliefs, such as "I'll never have enough" or "Money is hard to come by," block the natural flow of abundance.

- Identify and challenge negative beliefs: Reflect on the thoughts and messages you've absorbed about money, especially from childhood. Ask yourself, "Are these beliefs serving me or holding me back?"
- Replace them with affirmations: Instead of focusing on scarcity, affirm positive beliefs like "I am worthy of financial abundance" or "Money flows to me with ease." Over time, these new thoughts will shift your mindset and open you to greater opportunities.

3. Embrace an Abundance Mindset

An abundance mindset is the belief that there is more than enough wealth, success, and resources for everyone. In contrast, a scarcity mindset focuses on lack and competition.

- Visualize financial abundance: See yourself living the life you desire, free from financial worry. Imagine the ways money enhances your life—whether it's supporting loved ones, traveling, or investing in your personal growth.
- Be grateful for what you have: Gratitude is a powerful tool for shifting your energy toward abundance. When you express gratitude for your current financial situation, you signal to the universe that you are open to receiving more.

- Trust the flow: Remember that money is fluid. It may come and go, but the flow is constant. Trust that as money leaves, more will return, often in ways that exceed your expectations.

4. Develop a Growth Mindset Around Wealth

A growth mindset is the belief that your financial situation can improve through effort, learning, and smart decisions. It empowers you to see challenges as opportunities for growth rather than roadblocks.

- Invest in financial literacy: Understanding how money works is key to changing your relationship with it. Learn about saving, investing, budgeting, and wealth-building to empower yourself with knowledge.
- Stay open to opportunities: Whether it's starting a side business, investing, or pursuing a new career path, be open to new ways of generating income. Opportunities are abundant, and being receptive to them allows you to tap into new sources of wealth.
- Focus on value creation: Instead of fixating on how to "get" more money, ask yourself, "How can I create more value?" When you focus on adding value—whether in your job, business, or community—money flows to you as a natural result of your contributions.

5. Transform Your Language About Money

The words you use have power, and the way you speak about money influences your relationship with it.

- Avoid scarcity-based language: Stop saying things like "I'm broke" or "I'll never afford that." These statements reinforce a mindset of lack and can manifest as a financial struggle.

- Use empowering affirmations: Speak positively about money. Affirmations such as "Money flows to me easily" and "I am in a harmonious relationship with wealth" can reprogram your subconscious to attract financial abundance.

Here's an affirmation you can try:
"Money is a form of energy that loves to serve me. It flows to me abundantly, supporting my growth, my dreams, and my ability to contribute positively to the world."

6. Set Intentional Financial Goals
To attract financial abundance, you must be clear about what you want. Setting intentional goals helps focus your energy on what you want to achieve.

- Set clear, actionable goals: Define both short-term and long-term financial goals, such as paying off debt, saving for a home, or growing your business. Be specific about the amount of money you want to attract and what it will help you achieve.

- Visualize success: Picture yourself reaching your financial goals—whether it's paying off a loan or earning a promotion. The clearer your vision, the more aligned your actions will become with your financial success.

7. Give Back and Circulate Wealth
A key part of having a healthy spiritual relationship with money is understanding that it's not just about accumulating wealth—it's also about giving back and circulating your wealth in ways that benefit others.

- Give freely without fear: When you give—whether to charity, family, or your community—you participate in the flow of abundance. Giving without attachment or fear reinforces the belief that there is always enough.

- Use your wealth to uplift others: Whether through donations, mentorship, or supporting causes you believe in, your wealth can be a source of positive change in the world. Money's highest purpose is to create more good.

8. Money Loves You
Spiritually, money is drawn to you when you honor it, respect it, and use it wisely. It loves to serve you in your journey toward abundance, freedom, and joy. When you shift your relationship with money from one of fear or scarcity to one of love and flow, it reciprocates by flowing more freely into your life.

Here's a powerful affirmation to reinforce this idea:
"I love my life, and I love how money loves me. No matter what form it takes, money is energy, and with mine, she intertwines. Prosperity finds me daily, and abundance loves to serve me as I create, give, and grow."

Conclusion

Money is both a practical resource and a spiritual tool. When you cultivate the right mindset about money, seeing it as a form of energy, embracing abundance, and treating it with respect and gratitude, you unlock the flow of wealth into your life. Develop a healthy and intentional relationship with money, and it will support you in achieving your dreams and contributing positively to the world around you. Don't be afraid, money has your back.

You may not understand it yet but I am absolutely right when I highlight the importance of the words you use when talking about money. The language you use shapes your mindset, which in turn influences your relationship with money, and ultimately, how it flows in and out of your life.

The Power of Language: "Spending" vs. "Investing" Money

1. Spending — By definition, when we think of "spending," it often implies the act of using up resources or money with little to no expectation of return. It conjures an image of money being "lost" or "gone." The subconscious message here is that once it's gone, it won't come back, and this can create a scarcity mindset around money. In essence, we see it as a finite resource that is being depleted.

- Spending Root Meaning: The root of "spending" is derived from the Latin word expendere, meaning "to weigh out" or "pay out." In modern language, this has evolved to signify using up or exhausting a resource. Therefore, it often implies money being used without the expectation of return, reinforcing the idea of loss or depletion.

2. Investing — On the other hand, the word "investing" signifies putting money (or energy) into something with the expectation of a return. The act of investing suggests that you're putting resources into something that will grow and multiply.

It's an empowering term, and it cultivates an abundance mindset, where you view money as a resource that can circulate, generate wealth, and return to you—often in greater quantities. When you invest, you anticipate future benefits, which cultivates a mindset of expectation and prosperity.

- Investing Root Meaning: The root of "investing" comes from the Latin word investire, meaning "to clothe, dress, or surround." Over time, this evolved to mean putting resources into something with the expectation of receiving more in return, implying growth and enhancement.

Understanding the Shift:

- Spending limits the potential of money, creating a belief that once it's used, it's gone forever.

- Investing changes your perception and allows you to see money as a flowing, circulating force. When you "invest" your money, you're placing it into something that is meant to grow and benefit you in return.

By shifting from a spending mindset to an investing mindset, you're retraining your brain to expect abundance and circulation. Whether you're purchasing an item, paying for an experience, or putting money into savings, if you approach it with the mindset of "investing," you invite more prosperity into your life.

How This Mindset Change Impacts Your Relationship with Money:

1. Empowerment — When you use the word "invest," you reinforce that every dollar has a purpose and is working for you. You begin to make decisions that align with long-term growth.
2. Circulation and Flow — By seeing money as an energy that circulates and comes back, you break free from the fear of loss and scarcity. You understand that money isn't stagnant and can continuously flow in your direction.
3. Expectation of Return — An investment mindset teaches you to expect a return, whether it's in tangible monetary value or intangible benefits like joy, learning, and growth. For instance, if you invest in your education or self-development, you expect that this will benefit you over time, just as financial investments in assets do.
4. Abundance vs. Scarcity — Words shape energy. Saying "I invest" as opposed to "I spend" shifts your mindset from one of scarcity (limited resources) to one of abundance (multiplying resources). You believe there is more than enough to go around, and more will come back to you.

Practical Examples:

- Instead of: "I spent $200 on a nice dinner."
- Say: "I invested $200 in a joyful experience that nourished me."
- Instead of: "I spent money on new clothes."
- Say: "I invested in my confidence and appearance with these new clothes."
- Instead of: "I spent on an online course."
- Say: "I invested in my knowledge and future career with this online course."

In all cases, the word "invest" aligns with a mindset of growth, opportunity, and return, while "spend" aligns with a sense of depletion. Your words become a declaration of what you expect—so if you expect your money to grow, multiply, and come back to you, using "invest" is a powerful way to reinforce that energy.

Conclusion:

By recognizing the deeper meaning and energy behind the words we use, such as spending and investing, you begin to shift how you interact with money. It's not just about transactions—it's about understanding that money is energy, and when you invest it, you are choosing to circulate it back into your life with abundance. This shift in language creates a profound change in mindset and, ultimately, your financial reality.

Here are some simple affirmations to open yourself up to receiving money and welcoming abundance into your life:

- I am open to receiving wealth in all forms.
- Money flows to me easily and effortlessly.
- I welcome financial abundance into my life with gratitude.
- I deserve to be financially prosperous and abundant.
- I release all resistance to receiving money.
- I am aligned with the energy of wealth and abundance.
- I trust that the universe provides for me generously.
- I am ready to receive unexpected financial blessings.
- Abundance is my natural state, and I welcome it into my life.
- Money flows to me in both expected and unexpected ways.

These affirmations are designed to shift your mindset and energy, allowing you to open up to the flow of financial abundance. Repeating them daily can help reinforce the belief that you are deserving and ready to receive wealth.

Here are affirmations to help you unlearn limiting beliefs about money and relearn a new, healthier, and more abundant way of thinking about it:

Unlearning Limiting Beliefs:

- I release all negative beliefs about money that no longer serve me.
- I let go of the fear and anxiety I once associated with money.
- I forgive myself for past financial mistakes and embrace a fresh start.
- I release the scarcity mindset and welcome the flow of abundance into my life.
- I no longer believe that money is hard to earn or difficult to keep.
- I am not limited by the financial struggles of my past or my family's history.
- I let go of the belief that wealth is for others and not for me.
- I detach myself from the idea that money defines my worth.

Keep repeating these affirmations daily can help reinforce the belief that you are deserving and ready to receive wealth.

Specifically, they can help you unlearn limiting beliefs about money and relearn a new, healthier, and more abundant way of thinking about it and about yourself.

Relearning a New Way with Money:

- I embrace new, empowering beliefs about money and wealth.
- Money is a tool that I use wisely, and it flows to me effortlessly.
- I am capable of attracting, managing, and growing wealth with ease.
- I am open to learning new financial strategies that serve my highest good.
- Abundance is my birthright, and I claim it now.
- I believe there is more than enough money and resources to go around.
- My relationship with money is healthy, peaceful, and prosperous.
- I attract money in expected and unexpected ways because I am aligned with abundance.
- I am always learning and growing in my financial journey, and I am open to new opportunities.
- I welcome the flow of money into my life, knowing that it supports my goals and dreams.

These affirmations will help you reframe your relationship with money, letting go of old patterns and embracing a prosperous mindset that aligns with financial abundance and freedom.

Here are some powerful daily affirmations to help you heal your relationship with money:

Daily Affirmations for Money Healing:

- I am worthy of wealth and abundance.
- I release all negative energy surrounding money.
- Money flows to me easily, effortlessly, and abundantly.
- I attract opportunities that create more money for me.
- I am open to receiving all the wealth life has to offer me.
- I trust in the process of financial growth and healing.
- My financial needs are always met, and I am supported by the universe.
- I am a magnet for wealth and prosperity.
- I am financially free and deserve all the riches of life.
- I am at peace with having more money and using it for good.
- My bank account is growing every day, and I am grateful for it.
- I forgive myself for any past money mistakes and move forward with confidence.
- I am learning new ways to grow and manage my wealth with wisdom.
- Money is a tool that allows me to live a fulfilled and joyful life.
- I am aligned with the energy of abundance and success.
- I am open to new ways of receiving and creating wealth.

- I trust in my ability to manage and grow my finances.
- I release any fear, guilt, or shame I have about money.
- I deserve financial freedom and peace of mind.
- I am thankful for the financial abundance that is on its way to me.

How to Use These Affirmations:

Repeat Daily: Speak them out loud in the morning (day) or before bed (night) to set a positive mindset.
- Write Them Down: Journaling them daily will reinforce your beliefs and intentions.
- Visualization: As you say or write them, visualize the abundance flowing to you.
- Gratitude: Always follow up your affirmations with genuine gratitude for your current financial blessings, no matter the amount.

These affirmations are designed to help you heal, rebuild, and cultivate a positive, healthy relationship with money. Repetition will begin to shift your energy towards wealth and financial freedom.

Here are more practical examples of how you can shift your language from "spending" to "investing" in everyday situations. These examples will help you cultivate an abundant mindset and see money as a resource that can flow back to you, often multiplied:

1. Grocery Shopping
   - Instead of: "I spent $100 on groceries this week."
   - Say: "I invested $100 in nourishing my body and my family's health."

2. Paying Bills
   - Instead of: "I spent $200 on my electricity bill."
   - Say: "I invested $200 in maintaining a comfortable home environment with the energy that keeps us warm and connected."

3. Self-Care
   - Instead of: "I spent $50 on a massage."
   - Say: "I invested $50 in my well-being, relaxation, and stress relief so I can be more productive and healthy."

4. Buying Gifts
   - Instead of: "I spent $50 on a gift for my friend."
   - Say: "I invested $50 in strengthening my friendship and spreading love and appreciation."

5. Dining Out
   - Instead of: "I spent $60 on dinner last night."
   - Say: "I invested $60 in a memorable experience and quality time with my loved ones."

6. Education & Learning
   - Instead of: "I spent $300 on a course."
   - Say: "I invested $300 in my personal and professional growth to elevate my skills and create new opportunities."

7. Home Improvement
   - Instead of: "I spent $500 on fixing the roof."
   - Say: "I invested $500 in the safety, longevity, and value of my home."

8. Clothing & Appearance
   - Instead of: "I spent $150 on clothes this month."
   - Say: "I invested $150 in my confidence, appearance, and self-expression."

9. Travel
   - Instead of: "I spent $1,000 on vacation."
   - Say: "I invested $1,000 in creating lasting memories, expanding my worldview, and rejuvenating my spirit."

10. Car Repairs
    - Instead of: "I spent $400 fixing my car."
    - Say: "I invested $400 in my mobility and the reliability of my transportation, so I can continue moving forward smoothly."

11. Childcare or Education for Your Kids
    - Instead of: "I spent $200 on my child's after-school program."
    - Say: "I invested $200 in my child's education and personal development to ensure their future success and well-being."

12. Charity or Donations
    - Instead of: "I spent $100 on a donation."
    - Say: "I invested $100 in supporting a cause I believe in, creating positive change, and uplifting my community."

13. Subscriptions or Memberships
    - Instead of: "I spent $30 on my monthly gym membership."
    - Say: "I invested $30 in my physical health and mental well-being, which will benefit me for years to come."

14. Buying Tech or Tools
    - Instead of: "I spent $500 on a new laptop."
    - Say: "I invested $500 in the tools I need to enhance my productivity and create new opportunities for income and growth."

15. Investing in Others
    - Instead of: "I spent money helping a friend."
    - Say: "I invested money in nurturing a relationship, showing kindness, and supporting someone I care about."

16. Entertainment
    - Instead of: "I spent $40 on movie tickets."
    - Say: "I invested $40 in enjoying an experience that brings joy, relaxation, and connection with others."

17. Savings or Emergency Fund
    - Instead of: "I put money aside for savings."
    - Say: "I invested money in my future security and financial freedom, ensuring I have the resources to handle life's surprises."

18. Debt Repayment
    - Instead of: "I spent money paying off debt."
    - Say: "I invested in clearing my financial obligations, freeing myself to create more wealth and peace of mind."

19. Health Care
    - Instead of: "I spent $100 on a doctor's visit."
    - Say: "I invested $100 in maintaining my health, preventing illness, and ensuring a long, vibrant life."

20. Business Expenses
    - Instead of: "I spent money on marketing for my business."
    - Say: "I invested money in growing my business, attracting new clients, and expanding my reach."

Why This Shift Matters:

Each time you use the word "invest" instead of "spend", you reinforce the belief that your money is working for you, not against you. You cultivate a mindset of abundance rather than scarcity. This change in language rewires your brain to expect a return, and that expectation will manifest in the way you attract and manage wealth.

By speaking as though your money is an investment (even in everyday transactions), you attract more wealth, more opportunities, and more prosperity into your life. Your subconscious mind starts to view every action you take with money as a conscious investment in your future success and well-being.

Final Thought:

Language shapes our reality. When you shift from seeing your actions as "spending" to "investing," you open the door for prosperity and abundance to flow back into your life. This simple shift is a powerful tool in building not only a healthier relationship with money but also a more abundant and fulfilling life.

Say it LOUD:
I LOOK LIKE MONEY

Write your own afromations for money

Date:
Title:

Money Likes me

People wonder

How does she become part of

My beautiful life

She turns my dreams into reality

What does she see in me

The way she speeds up all of my prosperity

I said that she likes me

She likes to feel my hands and my fingers

She likes to feel my pockets, my bank,

And my investment accounts

She likes to be around me

She also trusts me and believes in me

I know she is mine and always chooses me

She says I am a magnet to her

I agree that we are magnetized

Today, I live a life better than my dreams

She shows up consistently and always earlier

Money is a woman so I am good to her

And she's so good to me daily. She likes me.

She helps me to rise in the right vibration

I am a powerful money manifester

I thank her for being there for me

She's a friend, she's a lover, and a fan

She's totally unafraid about

What others have to say

She simply chooses me

No matter where I am

Like a Spirit, she always finds me

I am so grateful for her

If I am not around or if I'm occupied

She simply waits for me

She even gives me the courage and support

To catch up to my dreams and purpose

I allow money to come and flow

Into my beautiful life and experience

I am simply grateful for Money!

Money you are welcome into my life!

Money Likes Me

I always get everything

I want and desire

Like some good food or a good friend,

Daily, she comes, she supports,

She helps and she rescues me.

I respect and appreciate her.

We have the best relationship.

Anytime I want something

She says just come and get me, or

Better yet, let me come to you

She helps everything else comes to pass

Easily, constantly, and effortlessly.

She flows to me under grace in

The most unbelievable and perfect way

I never miss a beat, I never miss a trick

She keeps finding me, I told you

I cannot hide from her, she likes me.

Together we are more special

Together we are so magical

Together we are productive and fruitful

Before I reach out, she's already there

I appreciate her so much in my life

She makes things so much easier for me

She provides the best and recognizes me

When no one else does or wanted to

She trusts me and gives me unlimited

access, She gives me the right of way,

Automatic priority over anything or

Anyone else in this world

She is part of my routine and night ritual

We get together every day and night

I'm so comfortable around her and

She is comfortable around me too,

It's official,

She likes me and I like her.

Money Likes me

When I tell them, they don't understand
They're fighting to not believe me
But, I also know that they know it's true
Money is comfortable around me, and
Even more around me than anyone else
She looks forward to seeing me and
feeling me wholeheartedly
As I look forward to her in my life
She propels me forward
So I don't focus on the past or
Any unpleasant situation
We're over any possible negative situation
Should it seem to you like
We did not fully get along
It was a total misunderstanding
But it does not matter now
We are perfectly together.

We are made for each other

We understand one other

We respect each other

We are so over it,

We are over the past

We are so good together now, forever

And for generations to come

We will only multiply and as always

We find our way back together

We have made up for life

We are good now and any other lifetime

No matter where, when, what, or who

We are good together for any dimension

Abundance is mine

Money likes me for real.

I don't care if you believe me or not

I believe in myself wholeheartedly

I know she loves me and I love her

Write your own afromations for money

Date:

Title:

Money Likes me

Funny how they thought

I was going to be up to no good

Yet here I am, up to the best

Of the best relationship with her

No more struggles, no more confusion

No more conflicts and headaches

No more heartaches and disappointments

Instead, it's just bliss after abundance

I am chosen and the best part is

Money is my very good friend

And everything else comes to me too

I decree and declare that I am good

I am a good person, I do good with or

Without money in my life

But I do better with money as

She gives me a bit more power and edge

Encouragement to do what I want to do

I am grateful for money

I have such a beautiful relationship

With money in my life daily

Money comes to me more than regularly,

Easily, constantly, and effortlessly

Money loves to feel my hands

Money loves to feel my wallet

Money loves to feel my purse

Money even loves to feel my closets

Money is everywhere I show up

Money precedes me, makes way for me

I find my shoes and I find money as well

I go to the kitchen, there money is too

I take a walk outside,

Money is already there waiting for me,

Money flows to me abundantly

Money chooses me like no other

Money not only loves me, she likes me.

Money Likes me

When money runs out of place to be

While others make her uncomfortable

She runs back to me, always to me

She trusts me and chooses me

In any given crowd, I can attract money

No matter how small or big, I attract her

She believes me and believes in me

Money loves my company

I enjoy her company, I respect money

No matter what form she transmutes to

Or what she upgrades to, first things first,

She always looks for me because

She yearns for my presence, and embrace

I can be in a stadium full of people

Money will recognize me, come next to me

Money stays with me and comforts me

Money expands me for my own good.

Money insists that I take her
Money wants me and flows through me
Money flows to me effortlessly
Money tells me that I am deserving of her
I have a phenomenal health and wealth
I always have more than enough
I am confident about my money
People love to invest in me
If anyone upsets her, she trusts me
Enough to tell me all about it, but more
Importantly, we get together,
And we help each other heal
Money allows me to do what I love
Like helping others and uplifting them
My ideas make perfect sense, so lucrative
People pay highly to work with me
Abundance is welcome in my world
Money is so comfortable around me
And I am comfortable around her.

Money Likes me

People don't realize that sometimes
Money changes form and when she does
She still finds me and I welcome her
No matter what happens, I know money
Will always come and be there for me
No matter when money changes form
I am the first to feel her presence
No matter where I go, she is there for me
I always have more than enough
No matter what is going on in the world
People are willing to give me their money
Because they know that money loves me
Sometimes, they're not at peace until
They share their money with me
Hoping to get some of my luck or comfort
I have an abundant mindset and life
I am conditioned to an abundant lifestyle

I have plenty of money for me and
For all of my endeavors, it's overflowing
No matter who it is or what it is
I know that money will find me
Money has no bounds, money is useful
Money has no limit especially
When it comes to me, money loves
To enrich me and keep me opulent
She comes to me in avalanches of
Abundance and I'm so grateful
The government gives me their money
Sometimes they don't know why,
But I know why, everyone loves me
And wants to fund me and my lifestyle
Money enjoys and loves to be next to me
People transcend to the other side and
They leave me their money
Even my pets find me money,
Money likes me, I experience it, I know it.

Money Likes me

I am abundant and have various abundances
In this life especially in health, wealth,
Success, joy, peace, happiness, opulence,
Serenity, fortitude, and so much money
I like money back because she never
backstabs me, she chooses me every day
When money needs a friend I am always there
Money finds her way to me every time
Just like an old friend, she knows her way
home and I am her beautiful and steady home
Money does not interfere negatively in my
life, she simply helps me, I am worth it
I am worthy of money, I am deserving of her
Money looks for me almost aggressively, if
I dare to invest a day without her in it
Money loves it when I invest her
She's spiritual and likes me unconditionally
Even when I spend her, she still comes back
to me in avalanches of abundance.

Money works for me and partners with me
She knows that I mean no harm to her
Or anyone else, money forgives me. It's just
sometimes I forget and when I do, she still
shows up in avalanches of abundance and
reminds me that she likes me forever
She recognizes me and I am familiar with her
I cannot escape her, she is all mine
I always have more than enough
I have a firm-sweet relationship with money
Money makes a vow to always be there for me
Whatever form is current and useful
Today and every day money is a good ally
I count on money and money counts on me
To circulate her all over the place
I have financial success and continued wealth
Money simply loves me, no other explanation
She is still comfortable around me even
After all these years, she still likes me.
More money is coming to me now, now, now...

Money Likes me

I know for sure that money is on my side

I can put on any mask pretending whatever

Money always finds me no matter where I am

She does not mind if I grow, she understands

Instead, she encourages me to grow

She likes it when I exchange her

To buy new things that make me smile, laugh,

and even giggle so hard at times

She likes to see me happy and comfortable

She likes it when I have all I need, want, and

desire; and all that I dream of having

I deserve money I am not embarrassed by her

I am now very comfortable with money

We have grown beyond the physical form

We are divine and spiritual too

Money loves to sit next to me to hug me

To embrace me, and to give me access to

All of the things this world has ever created

I have access to the most beautiful things

This wonderful universe has never known
Money keeps coming to me unconditionally
Money loves to see that smile on my face and
Loves to hear my laughter play out loud
Money finds her way to me always
I can make as much money as I choose to
Even the most ridiculous amounts come true
Money is real energy, she's my best friend
She picked me when no one else believed in
me, supported me, guided me, or inspired me
Money even sneaks into my dreams and
The next day it truly comes true. I like that.
I like money. I am abundant. I am rich.
I attract money, I am so wealthy
I inspire so many with my opulence
They love to see the way I enjoy life
And hope to be like that too
I live in a state of wealth money never ceases
A state of constant cycle of abundance where
Money likes me shamelessly. I told you so!

Write your own afromations for money

Date:

Title:

Money Likes me

I know just like a child gets hurt and runs back to their mother
Well money does run back to me every time
Because people are often ignorant or simply don't know how to treat her right
I know how to live an abundant life
I share my gifts and talents, I harm no one
There is so much abundance in the universe
I live in a state of richness and abundance
Everything I want and desire comes to me
I attract wealth and that takes away nothing from any other person or thing
My money is unlimited and money loves me
Some people have a scarcity mindset and make money sick by suffocating her
So money runs back to me and I make her feel better, I multiply her, I invest her, let her flow, I circulate her, I am financially blessed
When I am happy and money is overjoyed.

I have no limit when it comes to money
She likes me, so she's unlimited to me
I buy things that bring me joy and peace
I help others who are in need, want, and lack
I provide joy in my life and for other people's
lives, all that with money's help
Money loves it, she loves that, she loves me
She loves it when I multiply her energy with
other good things I also get to keep
This is why money recognizes me and
Keeps finding me because I get her
And she gets me, she keeps me abundant
I am in a truly committed real-lationship
with money and she likes that, she likes me
My mind believes me so
I say even better things about money
Money is never tired of prioritizing me, and
I am never tired of choosing her
And I welcome her every time, every day
I am so grateful. Money loves me.

Money Likes me

Money trusts me and respects me

I utilize money and respect her

Should money not feel too good

I am her therapist and most open confidant

I like to invest in her and multiply her daily

Money brings me good things and good luck

Money gives me access to even better things

And so many wonderful experiences

When I want to go to the shopping center

Money is already there waiting on me

I get all I need and they don't want my money

Someone already paid for me

If I desire something to eat like diner or lunch

Money makes the reservation and makes sure

that I get the best of the best experience

Though they give me the best of the best

Yet still refuse to take my money

They simply feel obliged to give me the best

When I want to take a nice trip

Money gives me an extravagant experience
Money gives me friends from all around the world, And even beyond this dimension
Money gives me the best of the absolute best of experiences, I'm grateful for the memories
I can do this for hours, days, and weeks
Money is embedded in my beautiful life
Money knows how to make me feel better
Just how to make me smile, laugh, and giggle
Money understands me wholeheartedly And never complains about how I circulate her
She knows my intentions are good every time, I never mean any harm to her or anyone else
I like money and I am not ashamed of it.
I make plans with money, we're a team
Together we are so positive and productive
Everything good comes to me
I am amazing, I am wonderful and wealthy
Money cares about me unconditionally
Money comes to me in avalanches of abundance regularly basis Thanks Money.

Money Likes me

Money loves me, and money likes me
Even when I go to places like the bathroom
I am still not alone, money still follows me
Even there money finds a way to get stuck on
the bottom of my shoes, money just loves me
I have unlimited access to money
Anything is possible for me
Money has no complex when it comes to me,
She will attach herself to anything that is
mine, on me, at my home, or the path I take
No matter where we are; she has no complex
She will fall on my shoulder like rain to find
Her way to me, money never hurts me.
Money always finds her way to me
She will do anything to get to me
She gets stuck under my feet, my shoes,
my sandals, or next to my car, and
she always ensures that I see her.
Money always finds me

No matter where I am, she finds me
I could be in the kitchen or the bathroom
In the bedroom, the library, or the garage
Money will find me
Money even attaches herself to my tires
Money waits for me on my trees,
under my trees, next to my trees
on the grass, in my garden, or by the garbage
On any ground I stand, or choose to walk on,
Money is already there waiting for me
Me and Money always have so much fun
All of the relationships with certain things
and people of this world may all go left but
money is right, she's always there
No complaints, she said she likes me
And I believe her. I like her too.

Money Likes me

Money brings me good energy

Good vibes and good karma

Also, she clears the negative energy or

evil eye that others try to bring into my life

Money is so kind to me

Money likes me and I enjoy her

I love money for what she does for me

Money loves me dearly because

I am a good Master,

I know how to manage and handle her,

She likes me and I enjoy her

Even in my dreams, money snicks in

Money thinks I have more money than her

Money is happy for me and all my successes

Money expects highly of me. She elevates me.

Money implants great beliefs in addition

To all of my wonderful beliefs

Money never abandons me

Anywhere I go, anything I am doing

Money is there for me

Money is my first supporter,

My first investor, and

My most supportive fan

Money is key in my life

And I am the key to her life

Every day I attract more money

I am so dope, so cool, and so brilliant

I can create money anytime and anywhere

When I go out to eat, some of the

restauranteurs do not even want my money

They are afraid of how my money multiplies

with me and that I look like money

They say my presence is like financial grace

The minute I walk in, they are all in awe

They all want to serve me like money

They offer me the best of the best

They can see money next to me, in my eyes,

on my clothes, and all around me.

Money likes me that's all.

Money Likes me

Let me remind myself of my prerogatives

First, I let go of what's not true anymore

So many things I said or other things I did

are no longer true for me so I let them go

I have a brilliant mind, I am so amazing

Money changes me for the best

Money upgrades me, propels me forward, and

Uplifts me today and every day

Money revives me to my true self and

Money shows me my real superpowers

If Money got hurt and was sent to

The hospital where I work as a social worker

If they told Money that she needed surgery

They go and fetch Money the best of

The best surgeons with five-star reviews

That is proven over the course of their work

Money would decline them all to pick me

No matter the pain, Money just wants

To be next to me, she wants to serve me.

If they prescribed her medication,
She'd still request me, I am her everything
I'm her medicine, I'm her cure, her addiction
Money loves me Money likes me She trusts me
She just wants to be around to help me
She knows I mean well, I am a perfect master
Money forced me to value myself
Money showed me my worth, I am worthy
Money told me that I am deserving of the best
Money is so happy to feel my hands and
My pockets, my jars, my cars, and my homes
Money even hides under my bed, she hides in
My shoe closets and my purse closets
She loves to hide in my vanity,
My walk-in closets and jewelry boxes
I always have to pay attention
Money always looks for me even if
I miss looking for her, she does not guilt me
She always understands me and precedes me
She is so forgiving, I told you she likes me.

Write your own afromations for money

Date:

Title:

Money Likes me

I rise up today oh I am grateful

I look forward to my days for my days are

Full of avalanches of abundance

I breathe health, success, wealth, peace & joy

Knowing that I speak Life in the Universe

Knowing that every single thing that

I ever asked for is coming to me now

Under grace and perfect way

Everything comes to me in divine order

I speak positively unto my life

I am my own self-image and my best friend

Now I know, nothing is too good to be true

Money is just perfect for me, never too much

Money loves me and surrounds me

Money believes that we look alike

But she's ready to serve me the most

Just like water, she has a memory

That never forgets, therefore,

She always remembers to keep me abundant

Every day,
Money finds her way to me
I have a very good, pleasant, balanced, and abundant relationship with her
Money is mine today and forever
Some may think that I am too much but
I have not yet even started
Money told me there's so much more to come, better than magic, deeper than mystery,
My money multiplies like the sand in the sea
Like the stars in the sky and beauties in a dream, money is magnetized to me
I envision our relationship to get better and so much better every day unapologetically.
I see money in my mind, then she lands in
My house, my bank accounts, my hands,
My pockets, my wallets, and my purses.
Money is never satiated when it comes to providing for me and making me happy.
Money likes me so much and it's so obvious.

Money Likes me

The Universe has put us together

Money likes me, she's in love with me

Money wants to have my baby

Money looks out for me

Money gives me better options that

I did not know were even possible in this

society, this community, or this world.

I get goosebumps at the amount of access

I have to today, I am in awe but I deserve her.

All the access I have is just because of money

Now I can get all of the things

I was praying for today and others

I was sobbing about yesterday

When people see me, they're speechless, then

They ask me for my spell, to know how

To bend money like that, They want to bend

reality and be friends with me and money too,

They think Money likes me and that

I am a god and they're not wrong.

God also but Goddess most definitely yes

I know my own divine power that

This world has never seen before

Perhaps I am both, I embrace my true self

But here I am standing tall

Also, simply King like Money

Money is so cool, my money is so sexy

She takes all the attention of the planet

I don't know but maybe

Money did put a spell on me, ensuring that

I am always abundant and comfortable

To the highest level that

I never even thought existed

or was possible in this world

I thought I was indebted to her but

She says she is the one indebted to me

I let her flow in ways she's never seen before

She gives me better than measly handouts

Confession time: Money likes me.

Money Likes me

I love to see the extra I can do because me and
Money are buddies and she cares, and I care
Money loves my family and all that's mine
Money loves my animals and my pets
Money loves my house and all its accessories
She uses them to bring me even more money
Money has a prerogative and it's to make me
so happy, loved, liked, and comfy
Money sees me and I see her, she trusts me
Money loves to make me happy, I trust her
Money loves to see me smile and laugh
Money loves to see me complete
Money loves to give me new, pleasant, kind
experiences, and lasting memories
Money loves to create wonderful memories
and beautiful watersheds in my life
Money loves to bring and attract good people
into my life and into my experience

Money keeps on choosing me
And never allows disparaging gossip about me, my life, or anyone around me
Money keeps toxicity so distant from me
She does not allow sabotage of any kind
Money does not play when it comes to me
Money makes my life easier and more pleasant, aspiring, and so much more beautiful, it's like she gives me more time
Money manifests in my life multiplied
Money was there before, she's here now and she will always be because that's the kind of friend Money is to me.
Money loves me and I love her.

Money Likes me

Money is custom made for my life

My life is free from conundrum

Money is used to come into my life

Money fits so well into my life

Like a perfect little green dress

Money recognizes me everywhere no matter

What country, continent or planet I am in

Money follows me like the best disciple

Money chooses me as a friend and a family

Money affords me the best life

Money magnifies who I truly am

and I am the most beautiful Divine Being

Even with the privileges I am still kind

My life is natural, beautiful, and dreamy

No one thought such a life, as mine, was even

possible until they saw me, I am a hero

I am the manifestation of money alchemy

Money makes me realize my powers

I have superpowers Money empowers me

To my true power, superpower, and my being
Money gives me more time in the world
Money attracts the best trips for me
Money attracts the best people for me
Money also gives me access to better people
with a bigger and better mindset
I am no longer invisible but invincible
Our love is enduring and natural
Our connection is so effortless and sweet
Now I only invest my time, never to be spent
I wisely invest my time with
People who know how to enjoy a good life,
free of pain, and limitations, full of love,
and full of dreams, passion, and purpose
Self-love and love for others,
friends or foes,
or plain strangers.
Money takes great care of me
And I am forever grateful.

Money Likes me

No matter what is going on in the world

Money still comes to me

Money says that I am her refuge

Money likes me unconditionally

Money brings me good vibes, even great vibes

Vibes that elevate me and uplift me

Vibes that remind me of who I truly am

Vibes to connect me to realms I did not know

I had access to in this lifetime

Vibes that remind me that I am royalty

Money reminds me that I am so much more

then what and who I thought I was

Money welcomes me into so much abundance

Money always acknowledges me no matter

who she's with Emperors, Presidents or Kings

She always says hello, hugs me, kisses me, or

simply flirts with me, she's so funny

Especially if I am alone, she's just goofy like

that, she loves to make me laugh.

Money wishes me well every day

And when it's my solar return

It's the biggest blast every time

Money says I deserve her

Money also desires me

Money is better than AI

Money brings me things faster than anyone

I usually say moderation is the key but with

Money, there is no limitation

She is open to giving me infinite resources.

Money does not agree with living frugally

When I can live like royalty, living so richly

with avalanches of abundance.

Write your own afromations for money

Date:

Title:

Money Likes me

Money doubles the pleasures in my life

Money makes me care even less about

what people think about me

Money also makes more people like me

But I am her favorite, no one compares

There are no words to express her adoration

I am flattered in ways words cannot express

Money helps me celebrate the way I want to

But not in any way I had to, I have choices

Today because of money I have options

Money makes me utilize every part of

my brain, my abilities, and my talents

Money encourages people to keep me in their

minds, their hearts, and their gifting list

I succumb to nothing but a great experience

Money sees me and rewards me automatically

Money embraces me and respects me

Money adores me and elevates me

Money makes room for me unapologetically.

Money shows up for me

Money brings me an exquisite ambiance

Money brings me access to good vibes

Money increases my access to an avalanche of abundance and impeccable experiences

Money brings me to different places around the world for the fun of it

In Some places, it feels like I've even discovered, like I've been there before

Making me believe that Money always liked me and has always been there for me

In the past, just like the present now

And of course the future

Thank you money

Told ya, money loooooooves me.

Write your own afromations for money

Date:

Title:

Money Likes me

I look so good and I'm so pleasant to look at

Money accompanies me as I enjoy life

Daily, I create new beautiful experiences

I govern myself and I do a good job of it

Money affords me better experiences daily

Money helps me gain better trainers

To impeccably train my body to its perfection

To train my mind to be the best of the best

To support my spirit in her journey

Money puts me in front of the best teachers

To place me at the top with the best of the best masters, Money supports me always

Money grows and multiplies to benefit me

Money encourages me to meditate and levitate

Money supports me to be artistic and elevated

Money enjoys when I go to shopping malls

To invest, circulate, and create memories

Money allows me to sleep more and rest well

Money affords me to sleep less and enjoy more

Whatever I choose Money is down with it
Money has my back and supports me
Money gets me good things, very good things
Money gets me to meet good people, legends
Money allows me to reach longer and farther
Than my arms and legs can reach
Money gives me the things I like and enjoy
Money is like all the community I desire
Money gets me to connect and reconnect with
better and bigger people regularly
Money likes me so much and it shows
Utterly in my life consistently.
There is no lie about it
Money truly cares for me and
I am open to receiving the great things that
Money is willing to offer me
Money allows me to reconnect with myself
She shows me that I am worthy
That I am worth it all
I am a true vibrant and living energy.

Money Likes me

Money makes me more interesting

She forces me to think more of myself

Money makes me even more irresistible

Money makes me more empathetic

Because I can afford all without troubles

Money forces me to heal myself

She forces me to look and analyze myself

To see things differently and more objectively

To see the true version of life, and of me

To let go of the illusions of suffering, pain,

Attachments, and aches, but to live fully

To understand my role in life

To awaken at a time it is so scarce

Money is a force that I can always tap into

Money brings me an environment to learn

unique skills and be exposed to my talents

to expand my horizons even bigger

Money brings me more ways to manage my

life and everything looks magical

Money is kind to me and respects me

Every day, I discover a new part of Money
Daily, I rediscover new parts of my own self
Regularly, I get to see my soul, my vital energy, I engage with my divine animation
No one can cage me in this world or the next
I appreciate, love, and care about money, and Money works so hard for me
Money objects and rejects toxicity entirely out of my life unapologetically
Money reduces nonsense in my life
Money expands my business opportunities
Money knows how to handle this world
Money is so dreamy and fantastic
Money qualifies me for better things
Money approves me for the best life
Money is like my double in this life
Money speeds up my delivery in business and Money speeds up manifestations in my life,
Money loves me and I love her.
Money won't cease to surprise me
I am so grateful for Money in my life.

Write your own afromations for money

Date:

Title:

Money Likes Me

Money facilitates my passion

Money does not judge me but encourages me

Money does not reduce me, or deduce me

Money lifts me up and holds me down

Whatever I need, money is there for me

Money stops me from being gullible

Money understands me, comprehends me

Money serves me and allows me to get

What I want and desire in this lifetime

Money gives me access to things, people, and

Place here and beyond that's limited to most

Money makes my life appear magical

Money permits me to study gods

Money gets me excellent trainings that

remind me that I can heal myself

That I am the Unicorn I have been waiting for

I am grateful for discernment and realization

Money gets spiritual with me too

Money gave me master keys to many doors

I'd like to open, and other communities
I'd like to be a part of
Money gives me access and keeps me occupied
So I don't have time to waste time and energy
And I don't get caught up in nonsense and
toxicity with anyone anywhere
Money supports me in looking forward
Therefore, I am always marching forth
Money helps me to stay laser-focused
Especially when I need personal time that
extends the usual time allowed in this
controlled society, in this matrix
Money helps me release trapped energies
That is no longer needed in my life
Anything that no longer serves me has to go
Money is so dynamic and unpredictable
Money is complementary to me
We match each other's energy,
Money likes me, I told you so.

Money Likes me

Money responds to me when I call on her

Money is always present for me

Money always supports me

I am never too much for her

Money always has room for me

I am always enough for money

She thinks I'm amazing and impeccable

Just as I am, no judgment, I am enough

She gives me room to grow or expand

Money is magnificent, intelligent, and fair

Money unblocks hidden talents and abilities

Money connects me with more conscious kind, sweet, and empathetic people in my network

Money helps me practice good things

Money grows my inner vision

Money makes it a safer place for me

Money gives me better closure than what I could have gotten from any other party

Today one thing I know for sure is I'm enough

Money rocks like nothing else in the world
Money helps me look even better naturally
Money is kind to me, so patient and true
Money accepts my invitation to be and
To stay present in my life
Money is my friend yet she's still a mystery
A mystery I live to embrace day after day
A mystery I look forward to every day
Money lets me in and moves up with me
Money elevates and upgrades me
Money looks out for me and inspires me
Money makes way for me when
It all seemed impossible
Money remembers me and rejuvenates me
Money loves to feel my hands, my life,
my heart, and my experiences
Money is a friend of mine today and forever
I have gratitude for money in my life
And money provides, loves, and cares for me
Money is good to me. Money loves me.

Money Likes me

I am free, loved, and deliberated

I am a loving and caring person

My life is different than it's ever been before

I met a new friend that cares for me and about me, day and night

She's always looking out for me

My friend is the best of the best

I have a new friend and she may be All the friends that I need

She gets me active in new activities

My friend is kind, sweet, and lovely

This friend is very important to me

Our relationship is our prerogative

Our relationship is imperative more than ever

Our relationship is impeccable

We are impeccable

We are open to new things together

We get to enjoy those new experiences

We compliment each other daily

Some may not understand it but who cares
Our relationship may be called an illusion but
it's more real than you'll ever know
I always have enough time and provisions
My friend makes me even more fashionable
My friend stimulates my instinct and genius
My friend makes me more confident
My friend improves my self-esteem
My friend drives me to a better life and
I am looking forward to more and even better
experiences as they come into my life daily
Money surely is my friend
Money makes it easier for me to be who I am
Money is so kind to me
Money opens doors for me
I welcome money into my experiences
Money loves to serve me and be there for me
Money walks and runs with me
Money is a great friend to have
Money likes me and I like her.

Money Likes me

Money does not disappoint me

Money fulfills me and satisfies my desires

Money grows with me

Money does cover me all day and night

Whatever I want and desire, money is present

My money is so tall and large

No one can count my money entirely

I get money in different forms

The amount is so much, it's limitless

It goes into the universe, and passes infinity

Money does not allow me to fail

It only provides the lessons to expand me

It gives me lessons on a tough day

And wonderful experiences on a great day

Money loves me enough to push me up

To push me forward instead of being stuck in

an unpleasant and detrimental past

Anything I want I manifest with or without

money and that's the magic,

Money precedes me.

Money Likes me

Money expands my energy field
for more and more abundance
First, she brings the garbage to the front
Then she burns it to the sky, then abundance,
and mana fall back from the sky
I always have more than enough money
Money helps me focus on my own circus, and
let go of other peoples monkeys, and matters
Money reminds me of my power
She only came because I called her and
I truly manifested her, I-manifested-her!
Money reminds me to let go of limiting beliefs
Or to simply never give it a chair when
it attempts to show up and visit where I am
Money is sweet and kind to me
Money is energized by me and I am electrified
by her, money fills me up with good energy
Money knows the right thing for me
Money is a good servant to have

Money works hard for me and only me
Money helps me to connect even more to
My body, no more lies about myself
I feel so authentic, I am authentic
Money helps me to reflect on myself and
To be an even better person, and bigger entity
Money is magical and mystical
Money keeps me in a nice headspace
I am such a nicer person than ever before
I am proud of me every day when I see
How much I am progressing
Money is superb and holds dear to me
She keeps me calm, relaxed, cool, and
collected, nothing disturbs me
Money invents things to keep me happy
Money loves to see that smile on my face
Money understands me without a word
She speaks to me telepathically
She amazes me constantly and consistently
I am open to receiving more abundance.
I am so grateful for money in my life.

Money Likes me

Money does change me, for today I am better

I am a much better character than before

I smile more and laugh consistently

I am regularly overjoyed and at peace

I am not cruel but I can defend myself and

I sure can get organic justice with or without

the system, the tribunal, or the legal system

I am intertwined with my ancestors' powers

Many lies were learned as I grew up but now

It's up to me to change myself, my life, and

especially my mind & all of me so I unlearned

I blame no one even for the lies and fake tales

Money showed me how to grow better

How to be a bigger man regularly

Even when I don't really want to

I keep the end in mind I focus on the prize

I am that Light, that Love, that Harmoney,

that Joy, that Peace, that New Story that

I have always been looking for

I am so glad I found myself
I am complete, I am whole
Money showed me that change can happen
and that I can grow to be better
Money helps me to have my own worldview,
I don't have to accept anyone else's view, or
Guilt myself because I am not like them
In fact, I am not like anyone else
I have ever met in my life
I am unique and special
Money never ridiculed me
She helped me escaped poverty
Money showed me that being myself is
perfectly fine and I don't have to be ashamed
or apologize to anyone or society.
Money loves me.

Write your own afromations for money

Date:

Title:

Money Likes me

Money showed me that things happen because sometimes in life, things just happen
She showed me that if I remain consumed of past matters and issues, it's harder to get over it, it's harder to forget it, and move on
It's harder to cross over the bridge while being afraid, doubtful, & remaining under it
Money helps me to be confident in my choices, my preferences, and my experiences
Money showed me more awareness
Money showed me to focus on the profit
In the spiritual realm, there are no lost
Money has real value for those who understand her. Money can save the world
She is invisible yet is around all the time
Money requires understanding and I get her
I possess money but I let her flow
I don't chain her or lock her up
That is why she keeps on coming back to me

No desperation is needed for her to come to me
Money helps me to help others around me
and around the whole wide world
Money makes the unreachable reachable
I know everyone can be a billionaire
I know because I am the blueprint
I am not afraid of money Money loves me
I do well with money in my pocket
I do magic with money in my bank account
I know about money so well that I forget all
I ever knew or learned about money before
They were all lies and myths of the past
Money supports me in loving myself more,
Loving my heart, my mind, and my life
Money helps me to design my life in
the best way possible and impossible
Money points me to the best routes and paths
So I can accomplish the things I desire
Money helps me to maintain a higher
consciousness no matter where I am.
I respect Money and she loves me devotedly.

Money Likes me

Money respects my inspiration and
all of my new aspirations
She allows me to keep what works for me
and I am free to drop what does not
Money showed me how to work hard and
play hard to maintain the balance, plus
I can do whatever pleases me, as long as there
is no harm to anyone, no damage in nature, or
disrespect to my Maker or our beautiful Earth
Money showed me that positive affirmations
to manifestations really work, I only need me,
and any help from anyone else is a bonus
Money showed me that life is pleasantly sweet
She erases my stress, anxiety, and worries
I am satisfied with money in my life daily
Money rewards me constantly, consistently,
unapologetically, and unconditionally
Money forces me to dream so much bigger
than I ever did before. She likes me.

My family is so happy seeing all of my money
They love to see how money loves me
Money serves me like no one else exists
My life unfolds daily like a beautiful dream
The most beautiful dream I ever had
I am always on the way to receiving more
money so I keep on expanding my territory
Money showed me that resistance does not
serve me so I let it go, I let it be, & I forget it
Money shows me, I can change my belief
to simply keep what works for me
regardless of what I was taught as a child
Money is one of the most fun energies and
The most magical experiences of my life
Money encourages me to remain authentic,
nonjudgemental, and to only concern myself
to please none but me, myself, and I.
It is so simple that it does not seem possible

Money Likes me

They don't believe me but they see the proof
Of money in my life and they are stunned.
Money simply loves me and I respect her.
Money makes me feel like
I am on top of the world,
She makes me happy & more confident
I know that any money problem can be
resolved completely & then absorbed wholly
Anything that's not pleasant I can let it go
immediately without lingering around to
collect more unnecessary connections, pain,
contacts, avoidable suffering, and aches
Money no longer allows me to beat on myself
instead she provides me with fancy,
bedazzled pillows to release my frustration
without hurting, damaging, or
harming any part of my beautiful body,
I am so grateful and so content
I am content knowing that money loves me

Now I can afford whatever I dream of
And I can dream of whatever I please
My heart never skips a beat when I invest,
move funds, and flow money around
I am so valuable more money comes to me
The government looks for me to give me
money regularly, pleasantly, and lovingly
Love is the channel for money
Respect is what keeps her coming back
Money is a woman She knows what she wants
She protects and covers who she loves
She provides for those who love her back
She's abundant to those who respect her
She makes way for those who are confident
Money makes things I desire cashable
Money removes limitations in my life
Money makes fantasies a reality
Money helps me get whatever I look for
Money brings priceless things to me
Money increases my power without any abuse

Money removes my headaches & heartaches
Money is a constant flow into my life
Among all of the things out there
I choose money & that's my final choice
With money hard work does not exist, not because I don't work hard but because working hard with money feels like a voluntary workout no matter how challenging it may be,
it is still delectable & so enjoyable
Late nights and long days are so pleasant
It's like hitting the gym while you're already healthy & in total exemplary shape.
I am so proud of myself, I am so grateful for effortless money in my life the way it is
My elevation is going to be meteoric
A story the world will talk about regularly, inspiring others for a long time to come.
Thank you Universe, thank you Nature
Thank you Money for trusting me.

Money Likes me

Money is not for hoarding & hiding

unless you're doing a treasure hunt

Money keeps me energized to create a better

version of myself & manifest better realities

Money showed me that manipulation can be

good as long as it serves the greater good of

the world, society, and humanity as a whole.

Money instantly clears ignorance, toxicity,

misinformation & gaslighting out of my life

Money reminds me that I have the power

to manifest, no matter where I am,

where I go, or where I will be.

Money makes me more pleasant & kind

I know how to open the channel to receive

All that I want and desire because

My channel remains open, kind & loving

I choose to stay activated & money supports

that unapologetically & unconditionally

Money helps me balance all areas of my life.

I never lose money, and I never miss a trick
Money constantly stimulates my imagination, expanding my wealth beyond what I can ever circulate, I always have more than I ask for
Money grows on all my trees - front, back, & even those I cannot see. Money keeps me awake with inspiration yet grants me deep, undisturbed rest, I am so grateful
I look forward to my days especially because I know I have money to resolve anything that comes up throughout my day or that of someone else, like friends, family, or plain strangers hoping for a miracle. I like money.
Money has more than love for me brazenly
Money gives me the opportunity to grow
The Universe ensures that Money supports me in all of my endeavors without limits.
Money makes me so much sweeter than ever
I give a million but I get ten millions back
I always get value in my investments
I appreciate it every time and enjoy it all.

Money Likes me

Money tolerates me, enables me to be my best
She allows me to be myself and deletes what does not work for me and my world
Money loves me and she likes me as well
The Universe is always expanding and so is my money always multiplying
I am grateful for my money
I am enough, I am always enough across all time, reality, space, dimensions, and realms
I am loved, I am able and capable
I no longer hide from myself
I don't cheat myself because I love myself
Money supports me in enjoying life
Money ensures that I am well-paid
The Universe ensures that I am paid
No matter the amount, no matter the time
I never lose a dollar or a dime
Anyone who tries to steal from me
Pays me back a thousandfold always.

Those who don't pay me back never find peace among the living or the dead
Money guides me to march forth
I don't need to look back
The universe, this nature leads my karma
The more conscious I become
The more forgiven and accountable I also am
Money is gentle with me but also
Money teaches me to be more responsible
So my actions are unapologetic, just, and fair
I am my authentic self unapologetically
I am no longer a victim
I am a survivor and a warrior
My money always pushes me forward
I remove all that does not work in my storage, my memory, and my mind
Money does not suffocate me, instead it makes room for me to make even more money, so I always have a choice to do what I want to do.
Told you, money likes me.

Write your own afromations for money

Date:

Title:

Money Likes me

Money allows me to be so much more creative about my experiences

Money allows me to create a new reality

Money allows me to set new and more beautiful intentions for me

Money allows me to have more fun

Money deletes any struggles and lets me know that Money is for me and I am exactly where I am supposed to be in this world

I always have enough money to do whatever I desire, want, and dream of

Every move I make is a money move

I never skip a beat, money brings me monies

Money helps me to like myself even more

Money guides me to buy things that build me Also, that provides long-term pleasures

Money makes me more unique in ways that Words can merely express how I am so exquisite, classic, demure, worthy unlimited

Money is obsessed with me because
I'm a match for money I know how she thinks
Money loves my company all of the time
Money never gets fed up or tired of me
Money just hands me everything effortlessly
I never lack anything or any money
Money does not break me instead it propels
me into new pleasant realities
Money tells me I never have to hoard because
I can always find money over and over again
I never lose anything or miss out on anything
in this beautiful life, in my magical world
I inspire and aspire others to do and be better
I have no room for poverty & limiting beliefs.
Money gave a new meaning to wealth to me
No one has ever been so comfortable with
money the way I am today, I am truly unique
I bring more value to money authentically
Money loves my high standards and
Money loves to fulfill them daily effortlessly.

Money Likes me

Money permits me to do good manipulation where I help myself and I help others
Money teaches me that I don't need to worry, most things have a price and come divinely
Money destroys whatever comes to harm me and anyone in my circle, money gives me that special power because I am that special
Money helps me to uncreate anything that's not good for me, that's toxic and unnecessary
Money makes taping into the Universe un-weird, blameless, profitable and so natural
Money is my superpower and I embrace it
I have so many means of enjoyment
I value myself, my life, and my money
Money boosts my full confidence, self-esteem, priceless supplies, lifestyle, and provisions
Money improves my vision in every way
I can see so much further now
Money improves my vision and dream

Each day money finds new ways to surprise me, and my environment. Money knows my energy signature, money is attached to me and always runs to me like a child does to their mother after missing them all day
Money puts priceless value on my life
Money recognizes my richest potential
Money is a savior, gatekeeper, and a rescuer
Money is a beautiful friend to have
She is so loyal to me. She is impeccable
Money loves me because I know her true nature, her heart, and her willingness
Money makes me do and accomplish today
Some things I never thought I could
Being who I am just makes me even more powerful with money. I am grateful.
So many good things get done in the world as money has habited with me and serves me with more money every day on a diamonds and rubies platter Money says I am deserving
Money helps me help myself. Money likes me.

Money Likes me

Money is not a requirement to life but it is a part of this life, a part of my life

Money is available and unlimited

Money is not hidden from sight or is it so rare

Money gives me access to unlimited wisdom & knowledge, to stay above the ignorant masses

Money does not give me time to think about things I don't want, or more negative things, events, and people in my life

Money reminds me that I am a good person

Money is always ready to create for me

The world could go empty, no more money but Except for me, money will find me

The government could try to erase money

Money will find new ways to get to me

Money will always keep her value to me

Money always worth more in my life

I know how to use her wisely and daily

She creates new ways to provide for me

Once a dollar reaches my hands its value multiplies, money knows my intention is to let her flow authentically and to augment her
I never have to borrow or steal money
She finds me and makes me a billionaire over and over even when society claims financial calamity, economic challenges, crisis, recessions, inflation, or embargo I never lack
The more I want, the more money comes
The more I desire, the more money shows up
Money does not dictate my actions but she follows my dictation, responds to my requests
Money is a great friend to have
Money is a wonderful addition especially
Because she is mysterious and so unlimited
Thus, making her one of the most powerful
Money empowers more gratitude regularly
Every day I am grateful and I feel wonderful
Money is consistent in my life
Thank you Money! I welcome you, I like you.

Money Likes me

Money unlocks new possibilities for anyone who has been through bitter moments and has known little pleasures from those who were scheduled to care and love them

I ask myself what I need to create to live a different life and I am ready to attract more and do more for the betterment of my life and that of my family, and humanity

I am not responsible for the world but I have a responsibility toward the world

Every day I plant new seeds with money

I do more to please myself not just to appease my thirst, I know myself, I support myself

No one knows me better than myself

I have plenty to share and spare. Overflowing.

I have access to maximum joy and I deserve it

Money ensures that I have unlimited access

Money is moral to me and I can make as much

I want and desire, I exchange money well

I provide real opportunities for myself and
for others just like money does for me daily
I negotiate well knowing that I already have
money in my pocket and on my side
I am never afraid of money, such a great tool
I comprehend and respect money
I respond accordingly to money, I let her flow
Money is a great supporter and fan
Money is honest, kind, and moral to me
Money is often misunderstood but I get her
I have plenty of money to care and spare
I like that I look for more and deeper in life
I have built memories for many lifetimes
I also create new routines to better my life
I built new paths to better new generations
and humanity included
I know I can do anything I put my mind into
I am worthy of love, health, and wealth
I look forward to more joy, happiness, and
possibilities that the universe has for me
Thanks for this awareness Money likes me

Money Likes me

Money helps me to focus on the things that
I need to be focused on the most
Money is no secret, but it's sacred
Money is energy and a sweet breeze
Money is fun but much more discipline
Money is unlimited and kind to me
I am consistent in my life, heart, and mind
I am a master manifester and a goal-crusher
Anything I think of, it manifests greatly
I'm always open to the possibility there may
be a way that things can change and get
better for me & Money has proven to be that
Money affords me all of the nice things I want
That this world has ever known and ever seen
I provide services that others love to pay for
I provide goods that others enjoy to afford
They're willing to pay more than what I ask
for. People find value in what I have to share
Money is my greatest energy She's consistent

Money teaches me more ways to make money
I don't stay stuck on things I want and desire
Instead, I imagine the possibilities of things expanding and money multiplying
Money loves me and loves to feel my hands, pockets, wallets, and purses
I am certain that life can always get better even after it already became better
I believe what I believe, money likes me.
My happiness is a consequence of money
My gratitude is a consequence of more money
So I get happy even if you see no reason for it
My gratitude is for everything in my life
Now my happiness is unconditional
My joy, peace, and wealth are unapologetic
My money just keeps increasing everywhere
I constantly have an overflow
I have more than enough to share and spare
I take the less resistant path
I don't fight I'm a lover and an alchemist

Money comes to me effortlessly and joyously

No matter when, where, or how young I am

Money is part of my legacy

Money responds to me promptly

Money looks out for me lovingly

Money protects me and my family

I am an inspiration because of my money

Money gives me a spotlight anywhere I go

I don't compete and I don't do jealousy

My life is more peaceful than I imagined

I am supported by money

I am supported everywhere I go

My life is filled with love and wealth

I always get what I wish for under grace

Nothing good escapes me, I attract wealth

Everything great comes to me I chase nothing

I attract the greatest pleasures of this world under divine order, in perfect way

I lack nothing, I miss nothing, I have it all

Life is good to me because of money.

Write your own afromations for money

Date:

Title:

Money Likes me

Money frees me from self-sabotaging, sick ideologies and negative habits

Money frees me from doubts and fears

Money is a great friend and supporter to have

I am worth it and a worthy master to her

My inner self tells me how to manage my money and how to make unlimited requests

Money helps me to live my life so much better

I am so abundant and prosperous

Money does not point out what's wrong

Instead she looks for what's right and helps me to multiply the positivity in my life

I am unlimited and so comfortable

I stand still and money deals, feels, and heals

Money's energy is bigger than anyone realizes

There is always more money for me

I keep flowing with life and I keep getting more and more than I could ever imagine

Money makes life so much more enjoyable

Money turns my I to a WE

So we are one agreeably and effortlessly

Money rocks and Money is the best

Money does not encourage fears and doubts

I breathe in prosperity I breathe out hardship

I don't care about other people's money

I have my own and I have so much more

I am chosen Money chose me over everybody

No need to summon, she comes unlimitedly,

voluntarily, effortlessly, and lovingly to me

I am comfortable with giving money to those

in need because they don't know who they are

yet So money supports me in connecting them

Money stays constant in my life like change

Even more constant than change itself.

Money may shock you but she surprises me.

I know the language of money I'm a master

When we are talking no one understands us

But we understand each other effortlessly

Money is not a worry to me.

Money Likes me

Money always comes to me consistently
Money comes to me in the form of checks, money orders, cashier's checks, crypto, gold, diamonds, rubies, oil, copper, land, and every other form spoken and unspoken, to harm to no one, under grace, ease, and perfect way
Every business and corporation feels like they owe me, therefore, they recompense me awesomely, I always harvest wonderfully
I always reap magical treasures and gifts
I am always celebrated and rewarded
Money reveals secrets to me, my best version
Money allows the ancient spirits to also whisper more secrets in my ears and head
Money trusts me and vows for me
I can flow millions and millions easily
It would simply feel like ten cents out of a billion dollars So my money is truly unlimited in my pocket, safe, and accounts

Money brings me sunshine at midnight
Money makes me more unique and confident
Money makes me right by being just and fair
Money does not need to humble me
Money collaborates with me side by side
Making everything works out so effortlessly
Money does not need to put me in check
I don't need to put money in check
I got her and she gets me effortlessly
Everything is always working out for me
No more delays but divine confirmations
No more struggles but infinite riches
No more poverty but promising wealth
Money comes to me easily, no more worries,
no more fears, and no more debts because
now I am abundant and a master manifester
I like and enjoy the way it all worked out
So many things going and I am not distracted
a bit, money has my back, day and night
Money is helping me to stay focused.
Money is like my (spiritual) basil leaves.

Money Likes me

Money gives me time to work on myself,
to work on my lifeforce energy
Money stays constant and present in my life
So many things I do and achieve in life is
because of Money, she is always a part of it
I know that my Power is within me and
I am always in control, I've got this!
Nothing governs my life but Law and Order.
I am at peace, full of joy, and so restful
I truly love myself even the parts of me that
seem unlovable, intolerable, goofy, and silly
Money customizes a unique abundance for me
Money reminds me I don't need to beg anyone
For I am self-sufficient & complete
Money is on point I don't need to question her
My words are my spells and they love me so
authentically and kindly, I am sovereign
Money always has wonderful messages for me
Money supports me in manifesting
Me and money work silently

I know who and what money is for me
Money supports my fearlessness & opulence
Money supports my breaking of soul-ties
Money makes room for me to grow and expand
Money breaks the negative spells and hexes
over my life, Every action I take is beneficial
for my internal and external life
I take intentional actions for my wellbeing
I claim my right, my strength & my energy
back to me, and anything else that was stolen
from me and taken with/without my consent
I claim my wealth, success, & prosperity that
were locked in places seen and unseen
I am here to get back everything that belongs
to me, I don't have to ask or beg, like a
magnet, everything is leaving its place
aggressively to come back to me wholly.
Money supports my self-love, self-care, and
self-sufficiency, and all of the joy for me
Money reminds me I am an ascended master
I Breathe. Money likes me & cares about me.

Money Likes me

Money likes me and tolerates me because

My Ancestors already paid and paved the way

I do my best to become better, and much better, and so much better than ever before

I can't stop loving myself and knowing myself better every day, it's addictive and attractive

I stay at my level, and I keep going higher and higher, every day I am so grateful

I respect myself, I handle my traumas and all the other things I've been through effectively

So today health, success, money, wealth, love, prosperity, opulence, and joy follow me like a magnet, no need to chase I always attract

Money gives me more than anyone else can

Money is honest to me regularly consistently

Money makes way for me happily lovingly

Money makes way for me authentically

Money makes way for me unapologetically

Money confuses my enemies in their poverty

Money is the Spirit I needed to hear from
I can talk to money for hours, days, and
years to come. We are connected divinely.
We never run out of things to chat about
Money and I are friends lovingly & peacefully
Money does not judge me or backstab me
Money takes part in my supreme grand rising
Money takes time with me authentically and
is patient with me unconditionally
Money allows me to be myself entirely
Society accepts me because I first choose to
accept myself regardless of what people think
or whatever they have to say about me
I walk tall not to undermine others but to
show that I've been through some stuffs but
I still conquered, I'm proud & I am still here
Money is proud of me & to be part of my life
I know myself, therefore, besides being the
most beautiful, I am the most dangerous
creature on this planet. I bow to no one.
I bind any misspells & bad spells right now.

Money Likes me

Money gets to witness my self-liberation
Money could write a book about me because
Everywhere I go, money wants to come with
me, to accompany me, and to serve me dearly
Life tried to weigh me down, but I won
All I requested for me, manifested irrevocably
I never have to explain anything to anyone
I request, I manifest, I get it, I receive all of it
I am open to receive what Divinity has for me
I effortlessly attract wealth and success
I open my mind, my heart, and my spirit to
receive all things for me in Divine Order
Money is that energy that accepts me
Money does not allow anyone to violate me
Money gives me a way to seek justice fairly
Money lets me color outside each line safely
Money permits me to get out of the box kindly
Money does not feel the need to punish me
Money gifts me more energy and power daily.

No one can take away the power money gives
Money helps me to vibrate even higher
Money gives me power to help the world
But this world, I am not responsible for
Although I have a responsibility toward it
Money does not make me work hard but
She encourages me to keep on working daily
Money supports my manifestations infallibly
I never lack prosperity, I accept the wealth
and abundance that the Universe gives to me
I am like a treasure hunter and a good one too
I find things that no one else can find or see
Money waits for me in all the four corners of
The universe and I welcome her lovingly
I am a magnet for great and wonderful things
Money is easy to find and Money likes me.
Money purifies my heart to be even kinder
Money comes to me in avalanches of
abundance, in multiplicity of richness
Money protects me from poverty mindset folk
Money assists and guides my manifestations

Write your own afromations for money

Date:

Title:

Money Likes me

Money brings more fulfillment in my life
I affirm my health, prosperity, and success
I manifest abundance infallibly and divinely
I deserve all the wealth and success I allure
I deserve joy, happiness, and peace I attract
I deserve to be admired and aspired serially
I breathe opulence every day as I continue to be wealthy, and wealthier every day, at every breath, and in every way so remarkably
Money flows to me effortlessly & abundantly
Money gives me access to crystal, pure energy
That's priceless and authentic to any world
Money inspires euphoric moments & freedom
Money increases my level of gratitude
I truly am forever grateful and content
Money has positive messages to me regularly
Money helps me keep my peace and harmony
I have no complaints about money in my life

Money makes my life more wonderful
I can easily tap into money's energy
To get whatever I am looking for or desiring
Money gives me unlimited access to her.
Money is constantly circulating in my life
I welcome money, health, harmony and peace
I receive all types of money in the mail, in various forms, like checks, money orders, cash, corporation and government checks, settlements, and fully paid coupons
I am worthy of peace, success, and prosperity that welcome me every day irrevocably
I am worthy of the joy that accompanies my success, health, peace, wealth, and prosperity
I am kind, polite, classy, and so opulent.
Money is a big spark of inspiration to me
Money has more money for me daily
My money multiplies effortlessly
When I need a friend support, I talk to money
I hand my burdens over to money, and
She gives me peace for my burden

Money keeps being nice and kind to me
Money is so good and pleasant to me
Money makes things possible and easy
Money swore an oath to always be there for me, no matter what people have to say
Money commemorates good memories with me
Money is always clear and honest to me
Money supplements what I missed in the past
Money overcompensates me lovingly kindly
Money gives me double the portion repeatedly
Always looking out for me consistently
Money makes me a more peaceful yet still
A major force to reckon with.
Money likes me.

Money Likes me

Dear Money,

I am creative,

so I create a better life

for myself and mine

I decided it's time to change

I forgive myself, I forgive others

And the passage for my money

became faster and faster,

better and better

I keep practicing over and over

and now I got it, I get it.

I understand and it's real

Forgiveness is a choice so today I choose it,

and my money is so comfortable with me now

It comes in a multitude of abundance to me

My words are full of energy of prosperity.

My words and energy create a wealthy aura

Money gives me good laughters and joy today

Money is significant to me now. She likes me.

Money Likes me

Daily I am grateful

because I see my life

and I appreciate my life

I am definite with my words

Everything I say is charged with energy

Full of unlimited abundance

I don't listen to others about my power or

What I can or cannot do

I simply trust my words and myself

I know this day I will get

My daily bread as I always do

And always will, I never lack bread

My words get me all I want and desire

I need nothing, I lack nothing but I have

everything. Money likes me so much

Every form of prosperity in this world knows

me & likes me. Money just loves to love me.

Money cares about me and cares for me

Money is constructive to me. She likes me.

Money Likes me

Here are some money healing affirmations:

1. I am worthy of abundance and prosperity.
2. Money flows to me easily and effortlessly.
3. I release all limiting beliefs about money and welcome financial abundance into my life and my generation-to-be under grace.
4. I trust that the universe is constantly providing for me and my financial needs.
5. I am grateful for the money I have now, and I am excited about the wealth & abundance that is coming my way.
6. My financial situation is improving every day, and I am open to receiving abundance from unexpected sources.

7. I am a magnet for money, and I attract wealth into my life with ease.

8. My financial success benefits, not only myself but also, those around me.

9. I am capable of managing my finances wisely and making smart financial decisions.

10. I am worthy of living a life of financial freedom and abundance, and I am taking the necessary steps to make it a reality.

Write your own afromations for money

Date:

Title:

Money Likes me

More money affirmations specifically for someone who may have started from humble beginnings:

1. I am deserving of financial abundance and prosperity, just like anyone else.
2. I release any limiting beliefs about money that have been passed down through generations, and I embrace my own financial power, and pass down a new financial power, and a renewed belief for my generation.
3. My ancestors worked hard to provide for me, and I honor their legacy by creating financial freedom and wealth in my own life.
4. I am capable of generating wealth and building a legacy of financial success for future generations of my family.
5. The color of my skin does not determine my financial worth or potential.

6. I am resilient and resourceful, and I can overcome any financial obstacle in my path.

7. I choose to focus on abundance and prosperity, even in the face of systemic barriers and economic inequality.

8. I am grateful for the financial opportunities that come my way, and I am open to receiving more.

9. My financial success is a form of resistance against the oppressive systems that seek to hold me back.

10. I am proud of my financial accomplishments and use my wealth to uplift and empower myself and my community.

11. I create my own environment, I defy every challenge and limitations set by society and others. I embody resilience.

Write your own afromations for money

Date:

Title:

Money Likes me

More affirmations about how money loves you and loves to serve you (personalized by saying I and ME):

1. Money is a powerful tool that loves to serve me in achieving my goals and dreams.
2. I am open to receiving money's love and abundance in my life.
3. Money flows to me effortlessly and abundantly because she loves to serve me.
4. I am worthy of receiving financial abundance because money loves me and wants to support me unapologetically.
5. Money is not my enemy; she is my ally in creating a life of joy, ease, and abundance.

6. I am grateful for the financial blessings that come my way, and I trust that money will continue to serve me in positive ways.

7. I release any negative beliefs about money and replace them with the knowledge that money loves to serve me and help me achieve my goals.

8. I am open to new and exciting opportunities for financial growth and success because I know that money loves to serve me.

9. I am in a loving and supportive relationship with money, and we work together unconditionally to create financial abundance in my life.

10. I trust that the universe is constantly providing for me, and I am open to receiving the love and abundance of money in all aspects of my life.

Write your own afromations for money

Date:

Title:

Money Likes me

Money helps me to see

where others cannot even see

and often abandon the whole process

because they cannot see or envision the rest

Everyday in every way

Prosperity finds me yes it locates me

Abundance finds new ways to love me

My words, energy and actions

Are charged with a great deal

of opulent energy that's unmatched

I lack nothing, I have everything

My daily bread awaits me patiently

I love my life unapologetically

I love how money serves me nonchalantly

No matter what form it takes or what I desire

Money comes to me unapologetically

Money is definitely energy and with my

energy, she always intertwines.

I told you, Money loves me profoundly.

Write your own afromations for money

Date:

Title:

Say it LOUD:
I LOOK LIKE MONEY

www.ingramcontent.com/pod-product-compliance
Lightning Source LLC
Chambersburg PA
CBHW062224080426
42734CB00010B/2012